CURRICULUM AND EVALUATION STANDARDS FOR SCHOOL MATHEMATICS

ADDENDA SERIES, GRADES K–6

SECOND-GRADE BOOK

Grace Burton
Douglas Clements
Terrence Coburn
John Del Grande
John Firkins
Jeane Joyner
Miriam A. Leiva
Mary M. Lindquist
Lorna Morrow

Miriam A. Leiva, Series Editor

NATIONAL COUNCIL OF TEACHERS OF MATHEMATICS

Second Printing 1993

Library of Congress Cataloging-in-Publication Data:

Second-grade book / Grace Burton . . . [et al.] .
p. cm. — (Curriculum and evaluation standards for school mathematics addenda series. Grades K–6)
Includes bibliographical references (p.).
ISBN 0-87353-312-7 (vol.) — ISBN 0-87353-309-7 (set)
1. Mathematics—Study and teaching (Primary) I. Burton, Grace M. II. National Council of Teachers of Mathematics. III. Series.
QA135.5.S393 1992
372.7—dc20 92-16408
CIP

Photographs are by Patricia Fisher; artwork is by Lynn Gohman and Don Christian.

The publications of the National Council of Teachers of Mathematics present a variety of viewpoints. The views expressed or implied in this publication, unless otherwise noted, should not be interpreted as official positions of the Council.

Printed in the United States of America

FOREWORD

The *Curriculum and Evaluation Standards for School Mathematics* (NCTM 1989a) describes a framework for revising and strengthening school mathematics. This visionary document provides a set of guidelines for K–12 mathematics curricula and for evaluating both the mathematics curriculum and students' progress. It not only addresses what mathematics students should learn but also how they should learn it.

As the document was being developed, it became apparent that supporting publications would be needed to interpret and illustrate how the vision could be translated realistically into classroom practices. A Task Force on the Addenda to the Curriculum and Evaluation Standards for School Mathematics, chaired by Thomas Rowan and composed of Joan Duea, Christian Hirsch, Marie Jernigan, and Richard Lodholz, was appointed by Shirley Frye, then NCTM president. The Task Force's recommendations on the scope and nature of the supporting publications were submitted to the Educational Materials Committee, which subsequently framed the Addenda Project.

Central to the Addenda Project was the formation of three writing teams—consisting of classroom teachers, mathematics supervisors, and university mathematics educators—to prepare a series of publications, the Addenda Series, targeted at mathematics instruction in grades K–6, 5–8, and 9–12. The purpose of the series is to clarify and illustrate the message of the *Curriculum and Evaluation Standards.* The underlying themes of problem solving, reasoning, communication, and connections are woven throughout the materials, as is the view of assessment as a means of guiding instruction. Activities have been field tested by teachers to ensure that they reflect the realities of today's classrooms.

It is envisioned that the Addenda Series will be a source of ideas by teachers as they begin to implement the recommendations in the NCTM *Curriculum and Evaluation Standards.* Individual volumes in the series are appropriate for in-service programs and for preservice courses in teacher education programs.

A project of this magnitude required the efforts and talents of many people over an extended time. Sincerest appreciation is extended to the authors and the editor and to the following teachers who played key roles in developing, revising, and trying out the materials for the second-grade volume: Angela C. Gardner, Ann Mills, and Debbie Mortimer. Finally, this project would not have materialized without the outstanding technical support supplied by Cynthia Rosso and the NCTM publications staff.

Bonnie H. Litwiller
Addenda Project Coordinator

PREFACE

Something exciting is happening in many elementary school classrooms! A vision of an innovative mathematics program is coming alive. There *is* a shift in emphasis in the teaching and learning of mathematics. Teachers are encouraging children to investigate, discuss, question, and verify. They are focusing on explorations and dialogues. They are using various strategies to assess students' progress. They are making mathematics accessible to all children while exposing them to the value and the beauty of mathematics. Teachers and students are excited, and their enthusiasm is contagious. You can *catch it* when you hear children confidently explaining their solutions to the class, when you see them modeling problems with manipulatives, and when you observe them using a variety of methods and materials to arrive at answers. Some children are working with paper and pencil or with calculators; others are sharpening their estimation and mental math skills. There is noise in these classrooms—the sounds of students actively participating in the class and constructing their own knowledge through experiences that will give them confidence in their own abilities and make them mathematically powerful.

> I remember my own experiences in mathematics in elementary school. The classroom was quiet; all you could hear was the movement of pencils across sheets of paper and an occasional comment from the teacher. I was often bored; work was done in silent isolation, rules were memorized, and many routine problems were worked using rules few of us understood. Mathematics didn't always make sense. It was something that you did in school, mostly with numbers, and that you didn't need outside the classroom.
>
> "My answer doesn't look like yours," my friend whispered, while glancing at my paper.
>
> "Yours must be right. I am not very good in math," I replied softly.
>
> "Do it this way," the teacher would explain while writing another problem on the chalkboard. "When you finish, work the next ten problems in the book."

We must go beyond how we were taught and teach how we wish we had been taught. We must bring to life a vision of what a mathematics classroom should be.

Rationale for Change

These are challenging times for you, the teachers of elementary school mathematics, and for your students. Major reforms in school mathematics are advocated in reports that call for changes in the curriculum, in student and program evaluations, in instruction, and in the classroom environment. These reforms are prompted by the changing needs of our society, which demand that all students become mathematically literate to function effectively in a technological world. A richer mathematics program is also supported by an explosion of new mathematical knowledge—more mathematics has been created in this century than in all our previous history. Research studies on teaching and learning, with emphasis on *how children learn mathematics,* have had a significant impact on current practices and strengthen the case for reform. Advances in technology also dictate changes in content and teaching.

Our students, the citizens of tomorrow, need to learn not only *more* mathematics but also mathematics that is broader in scope. They must have a strong academic foundation to enable them to expand their knowledge, to interpret information, to make reasonable decisions, and to solve increasingly complex problems using various approaches and tools, including calculators and computers. Mathematics instruction must reflect and implement these revised educational goals and increased expectations.

The blueprint for reform is the *Curriculum and Evaluation Standards for School Mathematics* (National Council of Teachers of Mathematics 1989a), which identifies a set of standards for the mathematics curriculum in grades K–12 as well as standards for evaluating the quality of programs and students' performance. The *Curriculum and Evaluation Standards* sets forth a bold vision of what mathematics education in grades K–12 should be and describes how mathematics classrooms can fit the vision.

I covered the apple with 7 square tiles and Carlos covered his with 12 goldfish crackers.

Mathematics as Sense Making

In the past, mathematics classrooms were dominated by instruction and performance of rote procedures "to get the right answer." The *Curriculum and Evaluation Standards* supports the view of school mathematics as a sense-making experience encompassing a wide range of content, instructional approaches, and evaluation techniques.

Four standards are closely woven into content and instruction: mathematics as problem solving, mathematics as communication, mathematics as reasoning, and mathematical connections. These strands are common themes that support all other standards throughout all grade levels.

A primary goal for the study of mathematics is to give children experiences that promote the ability *to solve problems* and that build mathematics from situations generated within the context of everyday experiences. Students are also expected *to make conjectures and conclusions* and *to discuss their reasoning* in words, both written and spoken; with pictures, graphs, and charts; and with manipulatives. Moreover, students learn *to value mathematics* when they *make connections* between topics in mathematics, between the concrete and the abstract, between concepts and skills, and between mathematics and other areas in the curriculum.

The Changing Roles of Students

Previous efforts to reform school mathematics focused primarily on the curriculum; the *Curriculum and Evaluation Standards* also deals with other factors—in particular, students—that affect and are affected by reforms. The role of students is redirected from passive recipients to active participants, from isolated workers to team members, from listeners to investigators and reporters, and from timid followers to intrepid explorers and risk takers. They are asked to develop, discuss, create, model, validate, and investigate to learn mathematics.

All children must be given the opportunity to develop their potential and the unique strengths each of them possesses. Set high standards for your students and guide them to attain them.

Many people, including students, believe that mathematics is for the privileged few. It is time to dispel that myth. All children, regardless of sex, socioeconomic background, language, race, or ethnic origin, can and must succeed in school mathematics. With proper instruction, encouragement, and high expectations, *all* students can do mathematics.

Your Role in Implementing the Standards

All elementary school teachers are teachers of mathematics. Thus, your role is to build your students' self-confidence and nurture their natural curiosity; to challenge them with rich problems through which they will learn to value mathematics and appreciate the order and beauty of mathematics; to provide them with a strong foundation for further study; and to encourage their mathematical ability and power.

The elementary school years are crucial in a child's cognitive and affective development, and you are the central figure. You structure class-

We used a grid 6 units wide and made a stripe design. Our pattern also makes stripes when the grid is 9 or 12 units wide.

room experiences to implement the curriculum and create a supportive environment for learning to take place. In most activities you are the guide, the coach, the facilitator, and the instigator of mathematical explorations.

- You give children the gift of self-confidence. Through your careful grouping, astute questions, appropriate tasks, and realistic expectations, each student can experience success.
- Long after they forget childhood events, your students will remember you. Your excitement and interest permeate the room and stimulate their appreciation for mathematics.
- Through your classroom practices, you promote mathematical thinking, reasoning, and understanding.
- You lay the foundation on which further study will take place. You give students multiple strategies and tools to solve problems. The questions you ask and the problems you pose can capture your students' imagination, arouse their curiosity, and encourage their creativity.
- You facilitate the building of their knowledge by giving them interesting problems to solve, which leads to the development of concepts and important mathematical ideas.
- Rules, algorithms, and formulas emerge from student explorations guided by you, the teacher of mathematics.

Tens	***Ones***
1	***0 1 1 1 4***
2	***3 5 7***
3	***6 8***

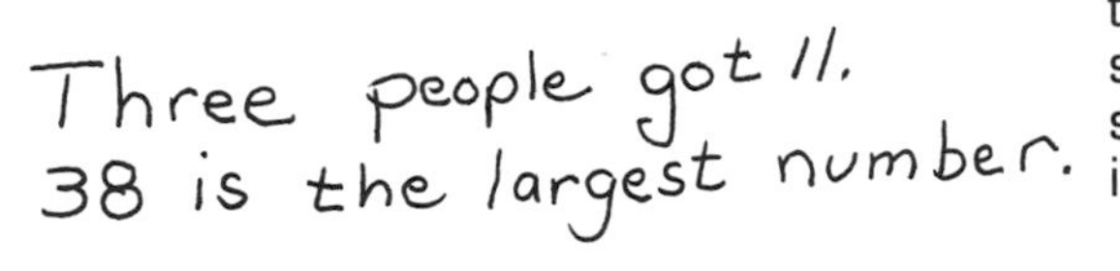

Instructional Tools and the Standards

In order to implement the curriculum envisioned in the *Curriculum and Evaluation Standards,* we must carefully select and creatively use instructional tools. The textbook is only one of many important teaching resources. Children's development of concepts is fostered by their extensive use of physical materials to represent and describe mathematical ideas.

Calculators and computers are essential instructional tools at all levels. Through the appropriate use of these tools, students are able to solve realistic problems, investigate patterns, explore procedures, and focus on the steps to solve problems instead of on tedious computations.

Implementing the Evaluation Standards

Evaluation must be an integral part of teaching. A primary component of instruction is an ongoing assessment of what goes on in our classrooms. This information helps us make decisions about what we teach and how we teach it, about students' progress and feelings, and about our mathematics program.

Where can you put the mirror so that you can see just two circles?

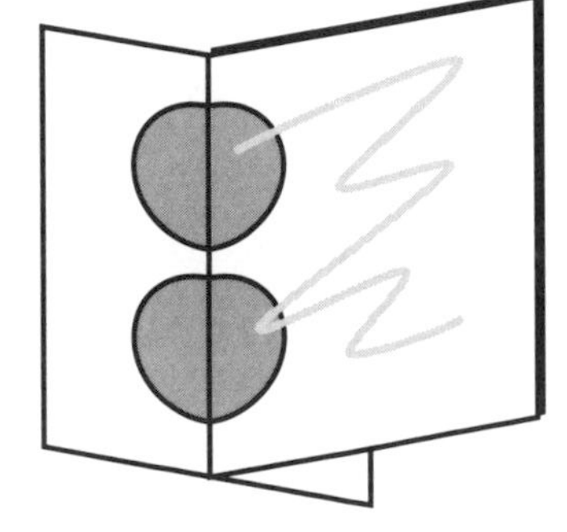

The *Curriculum and Evaluation Standards* advocates many changes in curriculum, in instruction, and in the roles of students and teachers. None of these changes are more important than those related to evaluation. We must learn to use a variety of assessment instruments and not depend on pencil-and-paper tests alone. Tools such as observations, interviews, projects, reports, portfolios, diaries, and tests provide a more complete picture of what children understand and are able to use. Knowing what questions to ask is a skill we must develop.

When we test, we send a message about what we think is important. Because we encourage reasoning and communicating mathematically, we practice these skills. Because manipulatives and calculators are valuable tools for learning, we promote their use in the classroom. Because we want children to experience cooperative problem solving, we provide opportunities for group activities. *Not only must we evaluate what we want children to learn, but also how we want them to learn it.*

"When students explain their thinking I can assess their understanding."

You and This Book

This booklet is part of the Curriculum and Evaluation for School Mathematics Addenda Series, Grades K–6. This series was designed to illustrate the standards and to help you translate them into classroom practice through—

- sample lessons and discussions that focus on the development of concepts;
- activities that connect models and manipulatives with concepts and with mathematical representations;
- problems that exemplify the use and integration of technology;
- teaching strategies that promote students' reasoning;
- approaches to evaluate students' progress;
- techniques to improve instruction.

In this booklet, both traditional and new topics are explored in four areas: Patterns, Number Sense and Operations, Making Sense of Data, and Geometry and Spatial Sense.

You will find classic second-grade activities that have been infused with an investigative flavor. These experiences include exploring reflections and lines of symmetry with mirrors and manipulatives; modeling slides, flips, and turns with physical motions; collecting data about the class and grouping by tens to reinforce place value; investigating the concept of probability; organizing data using stem-and-leaf charts; developing geometric and numerical concepts of even and odd numbers; discovering and validating patterns on the hundreds board; recognizing patterns as relations; and making the transition from concrete and pictorial representations of the patterns to verbal and written expressions. You will also encounter a variety of problems and questions to explore with your second graders.

My design has one square and four triangles.

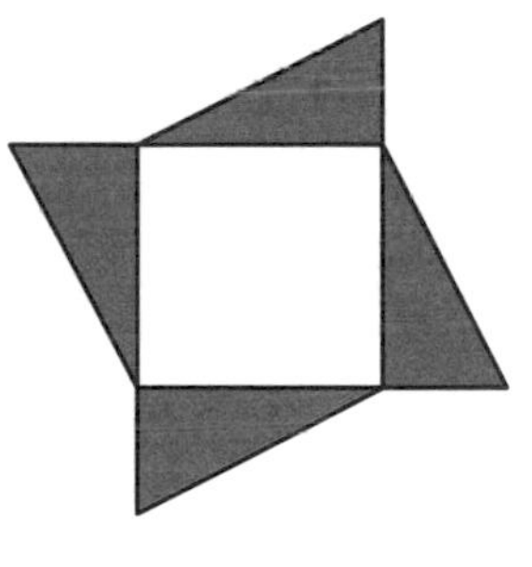

Change is an ongoing process that takes time and courage. It is not easy to go beyond comfort and security to try new things. As you use this book, pick and choose at will, and sample alternative approaches and ideas for instruction and assessment. Savor the freedom of change. All the documents in the world will not effect change in the classrooms; *only you can.*

With 6 square tiles I made a rectangle with two rows. So 6 is an even number.

The Challenge and the Vision

"I wonder why...?"

"What would happen if ...?" "Tell me about your pattern."

"Can you do it another way?" "Our group has a different solution."

These inviting words give students the freedom to be creative, the confidence to solve problems, and the power to do mathematics. When you give your students the opportunity to construct their own knowledge, you are opening the doors of mathematics to *all* young learners.

This is the challenge. This is the vision.

Miriam A. Leiva, Editor
K–6 Addenda Series

BIBLIOGRAPHY

National Council of Teachers of Mathematics. Curriculum and Evaluation Standards for School Mathematics Addenda Series, Grades K–6, edited by Miriam A. Leiva. Reston, Va.: The Council, 1991–92.

_____. Curriculum and Evaluation Standards for School Mathematics Addenda Series, Grades 5–8, edited by Frances R. Curcio. Reston, Va.: The Council, 1991–92.

_____. Curriculum and Evaluation Standards for School Mathematics Addenda Series, Grades 9–12, edited by Christian R. Hirsch. Reston, Va.: The Council, 1991–92.

_____. *Curriculum and Evaluation Standards for School Mathematics.* Reston, Va.: The Council, 1989a.

_____. *New Directions for Elementary School Mathematics.* 1989 Yearbook of the National Council of Teachers of Mathematics. Edited by Paul Trafton. Reston, Va.: The Council, 1989b.

_____. *Professional Standards for Teaching Mathematics.* Reston, Va.: The Council, 1991.

National Research Council. *Everybody Counts: A Report to the Nation on the Future of Mathematics Education.* Washington, D.C.: National Academy Press, 1989.

ACKNOWLEDGMENTS

At a time when the mathematics community was looking for directions on implementing the *Curriculum and Evaluation Standards for School Mathematics,* a group of dedicated professionals agreed to serve on the NCTM Elementary Addenda Project.

The task of editing and writing for this series has been challenging and rewarding. Selecting, testing, writing, and editing, as we attempted to translate the message of the *Standards* into classroom practices, proved to be a monumental and ambitious task. It could not have been done without the dedication and hard work of the authors, the teachers who reviewed and field tested the activities, and the editorial team.

My appreciation is extended to the main authors for each topic:

Grace Burton	Number Sense and Operations
Terrence Coburn	Patterns
John Del Grande and Lorna Morrow	Geometry and Spatial Sense
Mary M. Lindquist	Making Sense of Data

Our colleagues in the classrooms, Angela C. Gardner, Ann Mills, and Debbie Mortimer, are thanked for giving us the unique perspective of teachers and children. A special note of gratitude is owed to the individuals who served both as writers and as the editorial panel: Douglas Clements, John Firkins, and Jeane Joyner.

The editor also gratefully acknowledges the strong support of Bonnie Litwiller, Coordinator of the Addenda Project, and the assistance of Cynthia Rosso and the NCTM production staff for their guidance and help through the process of planning and producing this series of books.

Two NCTM presidents, Shirley Frye and Iris Carl, inspired us. A third president, Mary Lindquist, gave countless hours and creative energy to this project. The Addenda Series is a tribute to them.

The greatest reward for all who have contributed to this effort will be the knowledge that the ideas presented here have been implemented in elementary school classrooms, that these ideas have made realities out of visions, and that they have fostered improved mathematics programs for all children.

Miriam A. Leiva

PATTERNS

Mathematics empowers students. Because mathematics is in part the study of patterns, recognizing patterns and predicting what comes next are crucial problem-solving skills that children must develop early if they are to succeed.

Children at this grade vary greatly in their intuitive recognition of patterns. Some children immediately see patterns, whereas others recognize them only after their attention is focused on a pattern by the teacher or another student. Because seeing relationships and making generalizations are abilities to be nurtured, pattern activities should continue throughout the year.

Second grade is an ideal time to begin making connections between concrete or pictorial patterns and numerical patterns. For example, consider the concept of odd and even numbers that emerges as a child attempts to share candies with a friend. What does it mean to come out even? What happens when it does not? Many questions both within and beyond mathematics require an understanding of odd and even to solve. If I tell you that my house number is odd, you can tell which side of the street I live on. If I have two coins but an odd number of cents, you know that the least amount I could have is 11 cents and the most I could have is 75 cents. If dollar coins are allowed, the maximum is $1.25.

Activities in this second-grade book bridge the concrete experiences of kindergarten and first grade with the more abstract pattern lessons that engage third-grade students. The Stripe Paper Company activity explores designs that create new patterns; the hundreds chart activity helps students picture relationships. The magic function box encourages students to write about the patterns they discover and create. The first activity focuses on odd and even numbers and is the basis for a computational exploration in the Number Sense and Operations chapter.

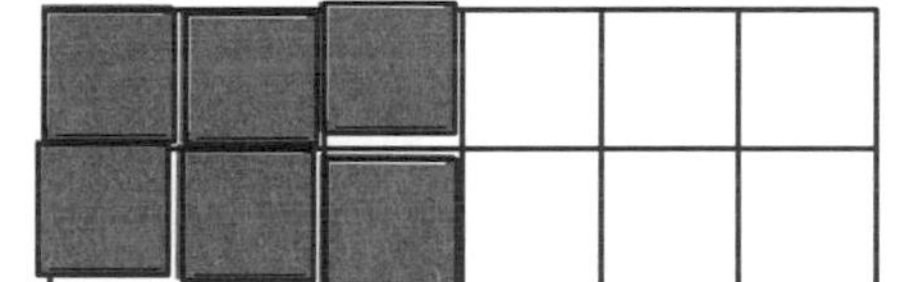

Rather than teaching children to memorize that numbers ending in 0, 2, 4, 6, and 8 are even, this activity develops the concept of odd and even by having students share tiles equally and build rectangles that are two units wide.

ODD AND EVEN

Get ready. The purpose of this activity is to have children better understand the concept of odd and even numbers.

You will need a supply of fifteen to twenty small cubes or tiles and a copy of the recording sheet Odd or Even (p. 6) for each pair of students.

♦ ♦ ♦ ♦ ♦ ♦ ♦ ♦

Get going. Have the students work with a partner and take turns being the recorder on the worksheet. One child picks up a handful of tiles, counts them, and deals them out to share them equally with the partner. The other child records the total number of tiles and notes if they were shared equally (no tiles left over). Have the children use the same tiles to try to build a rectangle on the grid at the bottom of the Odd or Even worksheet. Show the children that the rectangles must be two units wide. The recorder should note if the tiles make a rectangle.

Were you able to make a rectangle with the tiles?

Did each of you have the same number of tiles with none left over? If you did, this number of tiles is an even number. Otherwise, it is an odd number.

Tell the students to complete the chart for the number of tiles drawn. Have them continue the activity by drawing handfuls of tiles, experimenting, and recording their results.

Keep going. Reinforce the concept of odd and even through additional explorations.

How could you determine if you have an odd number or an even number of doors at home?

Remember that there are cupboard, appliance, and cabinet doors as well as standard house doors to be counted!

Is there an even number or an odd number of outside doors at your house? Do more students have an even or an odd number of outside doors at their houses?

Encourage the students to suggest other investigations related to odd and even numbers. For example, ask,

Do we have an odd number or an even number of teachers (or classrooms) in the school?

Is there an odd number or an even number of desks in the classroom?

NEW PATTERNS FROM OTHER DESIGNS

Get ready. The purpose of this activity is to have children analyze visual patterns. They will explore what happens when the same pattern units are recorded on grids of various widths. Students will write about and talk about what they discover. This powerful exploration leads to the concepts of grouping, multiplicity, and divisibility. If the pattern has three units, it will make stripes on grids whose widths are multiples of three: 3, 6, 9, and so on.

Prepare blank strips that are three, four, or five squares long. About a third of the class will work with each length, but you will want to have extra strips so that students may experiment before deciding on the one design they will use for the activity.

Divide the class into design teams of two. Each pair of students will need crayons and copies of the Stripe Paper Company worksheet (pp. 7 and 8). If you have an odd number of students, allow a student who enjoys coloring and works quickly to work alone.

♦ ♦ ♦ ♦ ♦ ♦ ♦ ♦

Get going. Read the following story to the class:

> *A new company that makes wrapping paper is moving into our town. The owner has decided to hire all of us to work in pairs as design teams to create patterns for a new line of wrapping paper. Mr. Stripe, the owner, especially likes designs that make stripes when printed on wrapping papers with different widths.*
>
> *Each design team will be assigned a length for its design. Some designs will be three squares long, some four squares long, and some five squares long. Teams may decide to color each square partially or fill it completely. Pictures or symbols may also be used.*
>
> *Mr. Stripe always gives these directions to his workers: "The first step is to talk with your partner about your ideas, experiment with some pattern units, and choose one design for your team. Next, you and your partner will color your design on the different widths of paper used by the company. Finally, you and your design partner will write a brief report for the company about your work."*

A writing assignment in which design teams describe what they did and what they discovered is a way to integrate mathematics and communication skills.

Give each pair of students several strips that are three, four, or five squares long. Together they are to decide on a pattern they will submit for Mr. Stripe's consideration. You may wish to draw some examples on the board to be certain that students understand the directions.

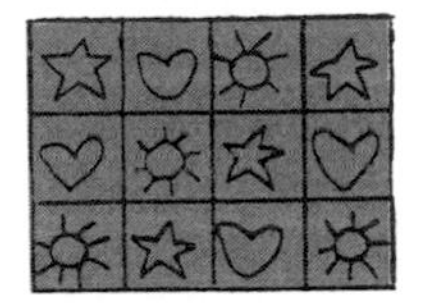

When the students have decided on a design, they will color their pattern on the design worksheets A and B. Always have them start the pattern in the square with the *. After they have colored their design worksheets, each team should write a brief summary of their work.

Why do you think that the same design looks different on the different wrapping paper samples?

Did you get vertical stripes on your patterns?

Why do you think you get vertical stripes for some widths of paper and not for others? Is there a way to predict if you are going to get stripes?

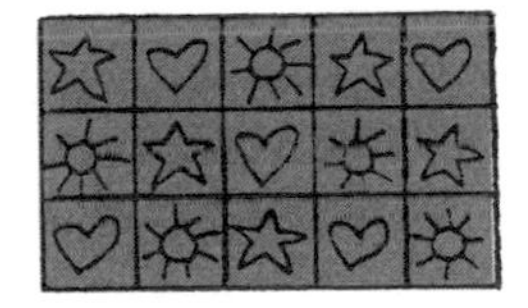

As the teams finish, allow them to compare their work and talk about what they discover. At the end of the lesson, post all design sheets and ask the students to examine them during the day so that the class can discuss them later.

Keep going. Encourage the students to look at all the designs that were created and to compare their finished samples with other teams' work.

What could you say about all the three-square designs as you colored them on the different-width papers? What about the four-square and the five-square designs?

When did you get a vertical stripe on the wrapping paper samples? Did any other stripes appear?

What did you notice about the wrapping paper that is seven squares wide? Since Mr. Stripe likes to have stripes on his wrapping paper but does need to have different widths available for his customers, what advice would you give him?

The students' designs and written descriptions could be used to create a hallway display so that students in other classes could observe the patterns.

As an extension of this activity, the students could design "signature scarves" with their names. Use centimeter grid paper cut into strips approximately 10 squares x 26 squares. The students choose a different color crayon for each letter in their first names. Beginning at the top left square, they write their first names over and over with the different crayons.

T	a	n	y	a	T	a	n	y	a
T	a	n	y	a	T	a	n	y	a
T	a	n	y	a	T	a	n	y	a
T	a	n	y	a	T	a	n	y	a

J	o	e	J	o	e	J	o	e	J
o	e	J	o	e	J	o	e	J	o
e	J	o	e	J	o	e	J	o	e
J	o	e	J	o	e	J	o	e	J

S	h	i	r	l	e	y	S	h	i
r	l	e	y	S	h	i	r	l	e
y	S	h	i	r	l	e	y	S	h
i	r	l	e	y	S	h	i	r	l

Does a pattern appear?

Color the squares with the first letters of your names. Which students have vertical stripes on their scarves?

EXPLORING PATTERNS ON A HUNDREDS CHART

Get ready. The purposes of these activities are to familiarize students with a hundreds chart, to identify some of the patterns found in this arrangement of numbers, and to practice counting patterns.

For the first activity, you will need a transparency of a hundreds chart or a large chart that all the children can see. For the second part of the lesson, you will need a copy of the Hundreds Chart (p. 9) cut apart into puzzle pieces for each group of students (pairs or small groups). In the final activity, each student needs a copy of a hundreds chart, twenty to thirty counters (for example, paper squares, cubes, or bingo chips), and crayons.

Get going. Display the hundreds chart on the overhead projector (or give each student a copy) and ask the students to tell you about it. As they state their observations, record the information on the board. You may wish to have the students color some of the patterns they identify to help others see what is being described orally.

What do you notice about the numbers in the last column? Where are all the numbers with a 3 in the ones place? Where are all the 0s? How many 0s are there?

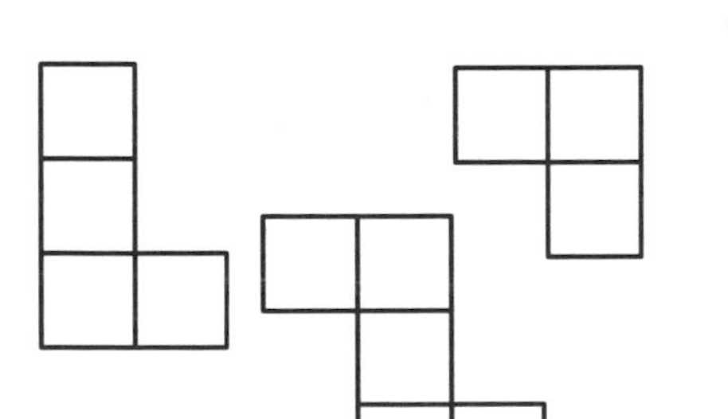

After the class has talked about the hundreds chart and has identified various patterns, divide the students into pairs or small groups and give each group a hundreds chart that has been cut apart. Challenge the teams to reassemble their charts without looking at a completed chart.

As the students try to reassemble the puzzle, you will be able to observe how different groups approach the task. Look for those who take the lead, for those who make plans rather than random efforts, and for those who are able to explain their ideas clearly.

Keep going. Using the hundreds chart on the overhead projector and shapes like those in the margin that you have cut out from plain paper, cover different numbers and ask the students to tell what is hidden. Notice that you can turn the paper cutouts in different ways as you cover parts of the hundreds chart.

How did you know what was covered up? Is there another way to figure out what I have hidden?

You could also furnish shapes with one number given and guide the class in filling in the missing numbers as shown in the margin.This challenging activity focuses on place value and counting concepts such as "10 more," "10 fewer," "1 more," and "1 fewer."

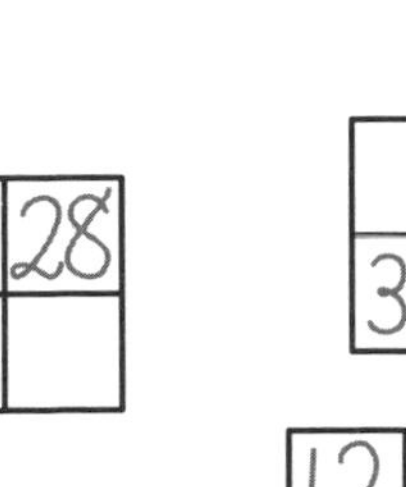

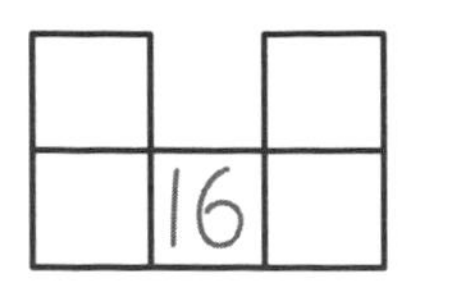

Continue using the hundreds chart throughout the year by focusing on skip counting patterns. Have the students cover their hundreds charts with counters or paper markers as they count by 2s, 5s, 10s, 3s, 4s, and so on. Let them record the patterns by coloring different hundreds charts and create a display of the counting patterns. Ask the students to go beyond what they have colored and can see.

If we extend the 1 to 100 chart, can you predict how each counting pattern will look? When we count by 5s, will we color 143?

♦ ♦ ♦ ♦ ♦ ♦ ♦ ♦

The students can explore a 0 to 99 chart to see if the patterns look the same as on a 1 to 100 chart.

THE MAGIC FUNCTION BOX

Get ready. The purpose of this activity is to have children move from the concrete and pictorial construction of mathematical patterns to a verbal and written communication of the patterns they recognize.

"Guess my rule" activities help students make the transition from concrete and pictorial representations to verbal and written expressions of the patterns they see. You will need a box large enough for the children to sit in (a paper towel box or an appliance box), index cards, and some markers. Help the students cut out the back of the box, decorate it, and fix slots for "in" and "out."

Encourage students to use the words "plus" and "minus" in place of mathematical symbols.

Get going. Tell the children that you and your partner (a student) have written a rule that the magic function box will use whenever someone inserts a number. Choose a student to write a number on a card and insert it in the "in" slot. Have your partner sit in the box and write a response according to your rule. If your rule is "add 5," a 12 will come out when someone enters a 7 and an 8 will come out if someone enters a 3. As you begin to use the magic function box, write on the chalkboard the number inserted and the number that comes out. After several examples, allow the students to talk with their partners and see if they can determine the rule that is being used. When a student tells the rule, have him or her use the cards that have gone through the box to verify the rule.

Keep going. When the students understand how to make the magic function box work, they will be able to create their own patterns and work independently. To prepare for taking turns as the person in the box, the students should write rules such as "add 4" or "take away 1" on cards. Encourage the students to write what they think the rules are and slide the cards into the box for verification. The students need to be able to tell and write the rules that describe what happens to the numbers when they are in the box.

ODD OR EVEN

Name ______________________ Name ______________________

Number of tiles	Sharing	Rectangle	Odd or Even
How many tiles did you pick up?	Do you have the same number?	Do your tiles make a rectangle?	Is the number of tiles odd or even?

STRIPE PAPER COMPANY

Worksheet A

Name ______________________________

Name ______________________________

*				

* Always begin the designs in this box.

Is your pattern 3, 4, or 5 units long?

Draw a sample of your pattern here:

*					

*						

STRIPE PAPER COMPANY

Worksheet B

Name ______________________

Name ______________________

*							

*								

*									

HUNDREDS CHART

1	2	3	4	5	6	7	8	9	10
11	12	13	14	15	16	17	18	19	20
21	22	23	24	25	26	27	28	29	30
31	32	33	34	35	36	37	38	39	40
41	42	43	44	45	46	47	48	49	50
51	52	53	54	55	56	57	58	59	60
61	62	63	64	65	66	67	68	69	70
71	72	73	74	75	76	77	78	79	80
81	82	83	84	85	86	87	88	89	90
91	92	93	94	95	96	97	98	99	100

NUMBER SENSE AND OPERATIONS

Emphasizing exploratory experiences with numbers that capitalize on the natural insights of children enhances their sense of mathematical competency, enables them to build and extend number relationships, and helps them to develop a link between their world and the world of mathematics. (NCTM 1989a, p. 38)

If children have number sense, they understand the relationship of numbers to each other, are able to tell when an answer or a unit of measurement is reasonable, and can use numbers effectively in many situations. Number sense takes a long time to develop; even adults continue to grow in this ability. To establish an environment that nurtures the development of number sense in children, you will need to provide interesting questions to explore, suitable materials with which to investigate those questions, and a classroom climate that encourages the discussion and the display of the results of mathematical investigations.

This bulletin board gives children a chance to show many ways to make the same sum. If they make large caterpillars, the children can use pressure sensitive dots to indicate the domino pips. The bulletin board itself is easily varied by changing the number on the caterpillar's tie or hat.

Although we may have experienced mathematics lessons in a passive way, research has shown that children learn best when they are active learners, trying new ways to find answers to problems and talking with their classmates about what they are learning. Many different materials can be used in these mathematical investigations: beans glued onto craft or Popcicle sticks, dominos, paper clips, small cubes, or just about any other easily handled item. Computers and calculators, pencils and paper, prepared worksheets, and student textbooks all have a place in the modern second-grade mathematics classroom.

The first activity gives children a chance to practice basic addition and subtraction facts in a problem-solving context. In the next activity, children use models of odd and even numbers to explore simple sums. A third activity encourages children to use numbers and words to describe relationships on a calendar. The final activity presents students with a chance to use manipulative materials to solve problems involving two-digit addition and subtraction.

♦ ♦ ♦ ♦ ♦ ♦ ♦ ♦

DOMINO CLOWNS

Get ready. The purpose of this activity is to have children find many different addends that give the same sum.

For each pair of students, you will need a set of dominoes, notebook paper, and a copy of the Domino Clowns blackline master (p. 16). If you do not have dominoes, you can easily make sets from 3" x 5" cards. Three dominoes, approximately 1 1/2" x 3", can be cut from each card.

Get going. Assign each pair of children a number from 15 to 30 and ask each child to find four dominoes that together have that number of dots. When they have done so, have the children put the dominoes on their clown as arms and legs. The children can verify their partner's sum and write on the notebook paper the number sentence that their own dominoes suggest.

Ask the children to choose another target number and repeat the activity several times. They will enjoy the challenge of discovering the largest possible sum that both partners can make using only one set of double 6 dominoes.

What would be the smallest sum that you could illustrate?

Suggest that the children use a calculator as they try to find dominoes that work.

Keep going. Later in the year you may want to use the Domino Clowns blackline master in an activity that focuses on renaming numbers and understanding place value. You will want to model the activity with the class before the children play alone. However, once the children understand how to play, this will be a good center activity.

Pairs of children have a Domino Clowns workmat and one set of double 6 dominoes. On each clown, the left side represents tens and the right side, ones. The object of the activity is to represent the greatest possible number. To play, the children turn the dominoes face down and draw them one at a time. Each domino must be placed as soon as it is drawn and may not be moved. As you model the activity, the children will discover that the number of ones on the right side as well as the number of tens on the left side may sometimes exceed 9. (For example, there may be 13 dots on the ones side and 8 dots on the tens side for a score of 93.) Since they need to name their numbers in standard form, some children may want to create addition problems.

Can you figure out your scores without writing down numbers to add?

Will you always have a renaming situation? [No, a clown may have 7 dots on the ones side and 5 dots on the tens side for a score of 57.]

Recording sheets may be used in a variety of ways. You can create four answer sheets from one blackline master. Ask questions such as these: How much money is in each cup? How much does each object weigh? How long is each ribbon?

Name ________	Name ________
A. ________	A. ________
B. ________	B. ________
C. ________	C. ________
D. ________	D. ________
E. ________	E. ________
F. ________	F. ________
Name ________	Name ________
A. ________	A. ________
B. ________	B. ________
C. ________	C. ________
D. ________	D. ________
E. ________	E. ________
F. ________	F. ________

ODDS AND EVENS

Get ready. The purpose of this activity is to introduce children to the patterns resulting from the addition of odd and even numbers. This activity builds on the lesson on pages 1 and 2.

Each pair of students will need twenty-one counters, two sheets of graph paper with large squares, scissors, and a single die.

Get going. Begin by asking the students if they could use their counters to model some numbers that are even and some that are odd. Have the

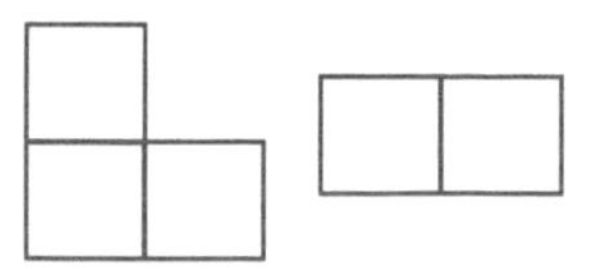

"I know that 2 is an even number because there are no blocks without a partner, but 3 is odd because one block sticks out by itself," said Katie.

It is important that children connect ideas both among and within areas of mathematics. (NCTM 1989a, p. 32)

students explain so that all children will be able to model examples. Ask them to use their counters to model all the numbers on their die and to group the models into odd numbers and even numbers. Each student should record the models on graph paper and cut out the six models.

even numbers odd numbers

Have the children take turns rolling the die and identifying the number rolled as odd or even. Tell the partners to add their numbers by putting their paper models together and to state if the sum is odd or even. Encourage them to roll their die several times and to model each addend and the sum of the addends, each time telling each other about the sum.

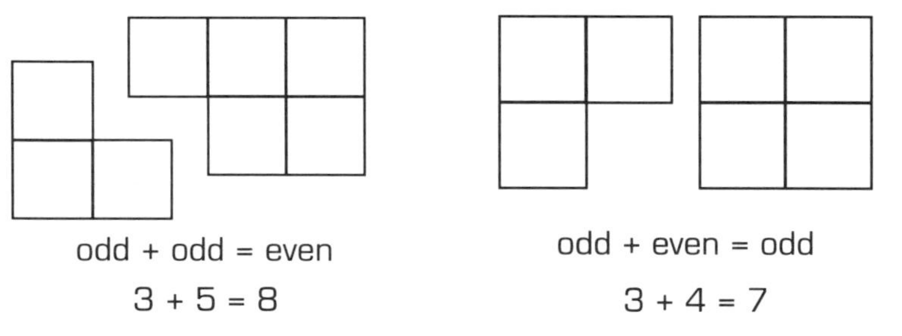

odd + odd = even

3 + 5 = 8

odd + even = odd

3 + 4 = 7

Addend	Addend	Sum
3 odd	5 odd	8 even
3 odd	4 even	7 odd
2 even	7 odd	9 odd
6 even	2 even	8 even

Keep going. When you are certain your students understand the task, have each pair make a table like that shown at the right as they roll their die and model the sums. After they have entered several lines in the table, ask them if they see any patterns and to describe what they notice. Suggest that they test their conjectures with other numbers. Encourage the children to explain in their own words their findings that the sum of two even numbers is even, that the sum of two odd numbers is even, and that the sum of an even number and an odd number is odd.

HOW BIG IS IT?

Get ready. The purpose of this activity is to help children discover that as the size of a measuring unit varies, the number of units needed to measure also varies. Through practice, we want them to discover that as the size of a measuring unit increases, the number of units needed to measure a given object decreases; as the size of the measuring unit decreases, the number of units needed to measure the same object increases.

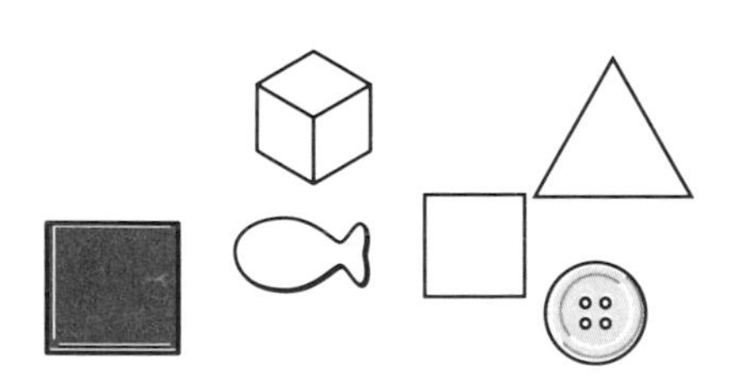

What I used	Guess	Test

Give each pair of students sheets of plain paper and ask them to draw around each other's foot. Then provide regular units of several kinds for students to use in covering one footprint. You might use paper squares, interlocking cubes, pattern blocks, or small crackers.

Have them make a chart with the columns labeled WHAT I USED, GUESS, and TEST.

Get going. Have each pair of students choose and record a unit, guess how many of that unit will be needed to cover each footprint, and record the guess. Now have the students cover each footprint with the unit, count how many units were needed, and record the number next to their guess. When the children have completed the task with several different units, ask questions such as these:

What unit gave you the smallest number? The largest? Why do you think that was so?

Keep going. Prepare a blackline master on which an irregular shape, such as that of a cartoon character or an apple, is presented. Have the students use a familiar unit to measure the selected shape. You might also wish to give the students other units and ask them to use the data they collected to predict how many of the new units will be needed to cover the shape.

After the children have explored with several different units, have them graph the number of each unit used. They could trace the units used on the horizontal axis and color in boxes that represent the number of that type of unit that was used.

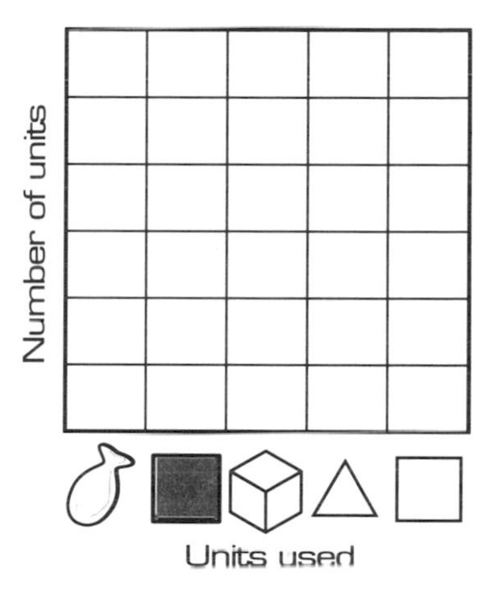

CALENDAR ACTIVITIES

Get ready. The purpose of this activity is to have children continue to develop mathematical vocabulary related to time and an understanding of time passage. In addition to your daily references to the date, you may want to spend some time investigating the calendar for the month.

A large classroom calendar is needed for daily explorations; for some activities, the students will need a calendar for the month on which they may write.

Get going. Routinely ask questions like these:

What is today's date? What was yesterday's date? What date will tomorrow be? In two days, what will be the date?

How many days are there in this month? What day of the week is today? How many more days until Sunday? Last week, on what date was Sunday? What date will one week from today be? Two weeks from next Saturday will be what date?

Ask the children to compare the number of school days with the total number of days in the month.

Which number will be greater?

What number should be added to today's date to find the date in exactly one week?

What two numbers could be added to get today's date?

Why is it not possible to have six Saturdays in a month?

Have the children draw a big X on the calendar to connect the days in two weeks.

MAY						
		1	2	3	4	5
6	7	8	9	10	11	12
13	14	15	16	17	18	19
20	21	22	23	24	25	26
27	28	29	30	31		

Assessment also must be sensitive to students' language development. As in any language, communication in mathematics means that one is able to use its vocabulary, notation, and structure to express and understand ideas and relationships. (NCTM 1989a, p. 214)

♦ ♦ ♦ ♦ ♦ ♦ ♦ ♦

Use your calculator to add the two numbers joined by the lines. What do you notice?

Try this again with other pairs of days. Why do you think you are getting similar results?

If you make your X bigger and add three numbers in a row, what do you think will happen?

Keep going. Encourage the children to create similar problems and solve each other's questions. Suggest that they look for patterns on the calendar as they create new puzzles and describe orally or in writing the patterns they find.

BEANSTICK ADDITION

Consider setting up a beanstick factory in one corner of your classroom. Students could learn about assembly lines, quality control, and working in shifts. Cover the work area with wax paper, since white glue will pop off the wax paper easily when the glue is dry. The power of this activity is in the process of the students' creating a place value manipulative.

By emphasizing underlying concepts, using physical materials to model procedures, linking the manipulation of materials to the steps of the procedures, and developing thinking patterns, teachers can help children master basic facts and algorithms and understand their usefulness and relevance to daily situations. (NCTM 1989a, p. 44)

Get ready. The purpose of this activity is to have children explore the effectiveness and usefulness of addition and subtraction algorithms.

Give each child a copy of the Addition workmat (p. 17), ten craft or Popcicle sticks, and a handful of loose beans. If you prefer, interlocking cubes can be used for this activity.

To make the beansticks, have the students glue ten beans on each stick with white glue. Let the sticks dry. Durability is increased when a thin ribbon of glue is applied along the top of the beans and allowed to run down onto the sticks and dry.

Get going. If the manipulative is to be useful, it must have meaning for the students. They must make connections between the symbols and the materials. Therefore, before the students use their beansticks to add or subtract, they need to use them to model numbers. Each beanstick represents a ten and each loose bean, a one. Have them model counting by tens:

Show 30; show 80; show 40.

Have the students then model the "in between" numbers:

Show 17; show 46; show 35.

Most students will show 35 as 3 tens and 5 ones.

Could 35 also be 2 tens and 15 ones?

Build a number on the overhead projector with beansticks and have the students tell what you are modeling.

If I add another beanstick, what will the number be?

What if I build 58 and add 6 more loose beans? Could I do any trading?

When you are confident that the manipulatives are meaningful to the students, ask two students to each name a two-digit number less than 50 (for example, 38 and 45). Then ask the class to make up a story in which these two numbers would need to be added. Record the problem on the overhead projector or at the chalkboard for all to see. Encourage the students to decide what the total will be and record all the answers.

Ask the students if their beansticks would be helpful in finding an answer to the problem. Call on several students to share their thinking with the class. Repeat the activity several times. No attempt should be made to restrict the addends to those that will not require renaming.

As children work with their beansticks and beans, encourage them to record each completed step.

Keep going. The following activity, which uses the Addition workmat, is more structured and closely models the algorithm for addition.

Have the students put three beansticks in the upper left box and six beans in the upper right box. Tell the students to write the number 36 in the recording box at the bottom of the page. Then have them put four beansticks and five beans in the lower set of boxes and record those numbers. Ask the students how they could use the beans and beansticks to find each sum.

It is important for children to learn the sequence of steps—and the reasons for them—in the pencil-and-paper algorithms used widely in our culture. (NCTM 1989a, p. 47)

Are there more than 10 loose beans? What could we do? How could we record what we are doing?

You may wish to have a child read the exercise aloud, *36 + 45 = 81*, while another records the number sentence on the overhead projector or at the chalkboard. Throughout the exercise, reinforce the concepts that the students are adding 36 and 45 and that these are not two separate problems in which they add 6 and 5 and then 3 and 4—as if the numbers all represented ones.

Suggest to the students that they extend the procedure to adding three-digit numbers. If you do this, have the students first make beanstick rafts by attaching craft sticks crosswise to the backs of ten beansticks, as illustrated.

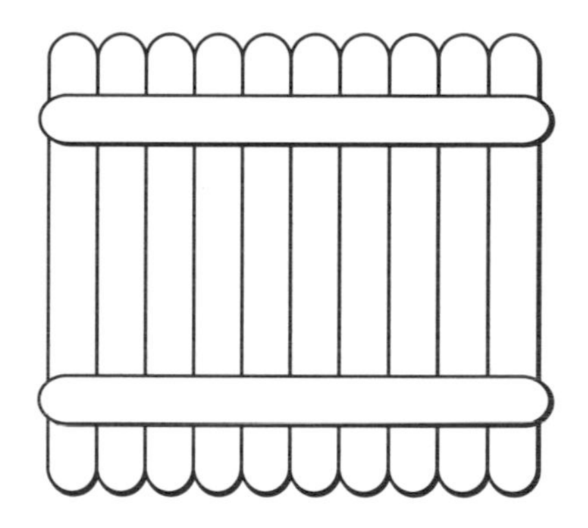

Beanstick subtraction can be developed in an analogous way. The recording sheet would look like the sample below. Ask the children to make up a story using subtraction. Have them put beansticks and beans on the workmat to model the story and write the number in the top section of a recording box. On the basis of their story, they should decide how many to take away and write that number in the bottom section of the recording box. Note that the number to be subtracted is *not* being modeled because it is contained within the original set. Encourage the students to explain in different ways how they would subtract.

(W)hen children's understanding is ... closely tied to the use of physical materials, assessment tasks that allow them to use such materials are better indicators of learning. (NCTM 1989a, p. 96)

What should we do with our beansticks to show what is happening in our story? How could we record this?

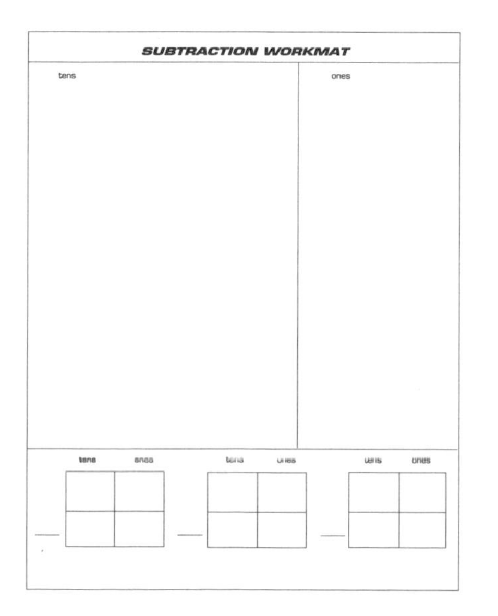

Domino Clowns
A
D
D
A
D
D

ADDITION WORKMAT

tens	ones

tens	ones

	tens	ones
+		

	tens	ones
+		

	tens	ones
+		

◆ ◆ ◆ ◆ ◆ ◆ ◆ ◆

MAKING SENSE OF DATA

Understanding place value is another critical step in the development of children's comprehension of number concepts. (NCTM 1989a, p. 39)

These activities, although emphasizing collecting, representing, and analyzing data, are built around place value and grouping by tens. The more second graders use grouping and place-value ideas, the more likely they are to develop a good number sense. As the children solve problems by collecting and analyzing data, they will be looking at tens and ones in many different ways.

Children at this age still benefit from using concrete graphs, such as those made with connecting cubes. These cubes are easily grouped into rods of ten to make counting larger numbers easier. Research shows that children do not easily switch from considering numbers in terms of ones to considering numbers in terms of tens and ones. The first activity is designed to assist with this transition. The students look at the same data in two different representations—first in terms of ones and then in terms of tens and ones—and discuss which way they think is the better way to display the data.

Children need to recognize that many kinds of data come in many forms and that collecting, organizing, displaying, and thinking about them can be done in many ways. (NCTM 1989a, p. 54)

Other types of representation introduced in this set of activities include opportunities to use paper ten-bars, a line plot, and a stem-and-leaf chart. Some of these ways to represent data may be new to children and new even to you. You will find the line plot and the stem-and-leaf chart easy and efficient ways to collect class data.

Probability ideas and language can be developed at this level as children make predictions about outcomes. As the children collect data about their experiments, they will need some ways to organize the data. This need connects probability to the experiences that children have had with charts and graphs.

WHAT COLORS ARE WE WEARING?

Get ready. The purpose of this activity is to have children solve a problem about the colors they are wearing. To solve the problem, the children will work together to gather the information and use connecting cubes to make graphs.

For this activity, the children will need connecting cubes in a variety of colors. Put the cubes in strategic places around the room, so that all the children have easy access to them.

Children often think that mathematics has nothing to do with real life because the problems encountered in mathematics class are clean and neat, but the problems in real life are often messy. It is not too early for children to realize they have to help define problems by making decisions.

Get going. Present the problem to the children in such a way that they want to solve it:

I have on blue shoes, a red skirt, a blue and red blouse, and a green scarf. I am going to make a color rod to represent me. A blue cube for my shoes and my blouse, a red cube for my blouse and my skirt, and a green cube for my scarf. Oh, I don't have a cube the color of my purple sweater, so I won't include it.

Then pose this question:

How many colors (the colors of the cubes) *are we all wearing?*

Let the children discuss what the question means. Should they count all the bits of color in their shoelaces? What about their buttons— do they count those colors? What if one child has a light blue fox and a dark blue elephant on her T-shirt. Do they count those as different blues? Take stock of how colorfully the children are dressed. You will probably have enough data if only clothing and shoes are counted but not bracelets, buttons, and so on.

Look for a unique characteristic for each child, so that every child has a chance to be the special one. Even little things like this can help children feel good about mathematics.

Pair the children so they can help each other. Have them get one connecting cube for each color, for example, a red cube for a red dress. When all the children have finished matching their own colors and making their color rods, discuss what they found.

How many of you had only one color? What color was it? Is that your favorite color?

Who had three colors?

Did anyone have more than five different colors?

Who had the fewest colors? Who had the fewest cubes?

Answering questions about individuals was easy when each had a rod, but this representation does not help much when the question is about the class as a whole. How we represent data depends on what question we want to answer.

At this point, you could save the multicolored rods and finish the activity the next day. Remind the children of the original question: How many of each color do you think we have on our clothes? This will be difficult to answer from the rods because they match the children and the colors are not organized.

See if they can tell by looking at the color rods for each child. Let the children suggest sorting by color. Give each group a color to collect and sort. Have the children, some or all, make rods of ten cubes of each color. When they have finished, place all the rods on a table as shown. Discuss what they found:

Which color appeared most?

Why do you think it did?

What if we only made color rods of clothes above our waists? Do you think blue would still be the most popular color?

If we do this tomorrow, do you think we will have the same results?

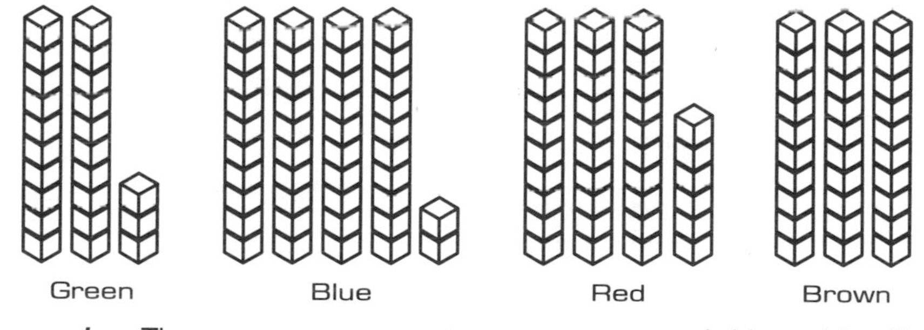

Keep going. There are many ways to repeat or extend this activity. If the children are really interested in whether they will have the same results tomorrow, record the number of each color on the board. The next day, have them quickly make their color rods as soon as they arrive at school or in some free moment. A small group of children could complete the sorting and make the concrete graph. Save class time for the discussion.

The way you manage this part of the activity depends on your style of teaching. One teacher put a piece of construction paper, one for each color, on desks around the room and had the children drop off their cubes on the matching color paper.

Change the subject—use colors of book covers, colors on bulletin boards, or colors in their mathematics books (divide the book so each child has about ten pages). Best of all, let the children decide what question they want to answer.

LETTERS, LETTERS, AND MORE LETTERS

Get ready. The purpose of this activity is to have children explore the number of letters in the names of small groups of children.

You will need three sheets of the paper ten-bars (p. 00) for each group of four students, scissors, tape, and crayons or markers. Give each group a number or a name. Have a place to display the results, such as on a bulletin board.

Get going. Ask the children to estimate the number of letters in the first and last names of everyone in their group. Record their estimates for discussion later.

Have the children cut out the bars on the blackline master, tape the groups of five-bars together to make ten-bars, and tape a white ten-bar next to a gray ten-bar until they have at least four ten-bars. (They may need more, depending on how long their names are.) Show them how to record their names, one letter in each box. Each child, with a different-colored crayon, should begin where the previous child ended.

JANAJONESWILLIAMBELLLatishaMasonMariaFuentes
BenCohenMidoriNakamuraJoWaltonDAVIDLEE
OmarShihobCOLETTEBOYERMaryCoxKevinO'Grady
LisaWinstonMohammedSaidTODDMURRAYAnneMiller
TYlerEVANSSaraGreenTomPaulosJanNelson
NANSKRYPNEKKeishaSimmonsMANUELSIMASThomasChan

When the graphs are completed, discuss what the children found:

How many tens and ones did each group use?

How did your estimate compare with the actual number of letters?

Were there any groups that had the same numbers of tens, the same number of ones, or the same total number?

Which group had the fewest letters? Did this group also have the person with the shortest name?

A teacher who had twenty-six students in his class made two groups of three and five groups of four. He let the groups of three pick one more name to use so that each group had four names.

Children doing this activity naturally choose a color of crayon that they like. The different colors make each name stand out.

One class of children decided to make graphs with cubes. They soon realized that they could not tell whose name was represented, but they could tell which group had the most letters in all.

When the children wrote about what they found in the charts, there were many surprises. The teacher remarked that she had no idea there were as many ways to look at this information as the children found. One student wrote, "I am the only one in the class that has double letters in my first and last names."

♦ ♦ ♦ ♦ ♦ ♦ ♦ ♦

Could we have made graphs with the cubes like we did in the last activity? What information would we have lost? What questions could we still answer?

Keep going. Children may like to investigate their findings by asking other questions: Which letter was used the most? Was every letter of the alphabet used? What was the length of each person's name? Have the children write about what they find.

One teacher said, "This is a game that I have a few of my students play in the quiet corner on a small piece of rug while I work with others. They often change the size of the target. We also made this rule: if a coin goes off the rug, they must also remove a coin from the target."

PENNIES AND DIMES—HOW MANY TIMES?

Get ready. The purpose of this activity is to have children play a game in which they record dimes and pennies in a chart that easily shows who had more of each coin in each round of the game. Recording their data serves as an introduction to stem-and-leaf charts, which are used in the What Number? activity on page 22.

Each pair of students will need nine pennies and nine dimes (real or play), a recording sheet for each child like the one illustrated, a space on the floor (carpeted preferred), and a target (a piece of paper will do). Have a calculator available for the grand total.

D	P
6	4
4	4

Students catch on quickly to this game. Show a few students how to play and let them teach the others.

Get going. Play the game with one student. Put all eighteen coins in your hand, and gently drop them onto the target. (You will need to experiment to find the height from which to drop the coins.) Record only the number of coins that land on the target. Put the number of dimes under the D and the number of pennies under the P for each drop. Take, say, five turns, recording the results each time on your score sheet. The winner can be determined in different ways. Keep it simple at first—whoever got the most money in each round is the winner for that round. Have the children find how much money they got on the target.

Keep going. Let the children decide on other rules and scoring procedures. Some children may decide that points need to be given according to the number of coins as well as their value.

One child felt that it was unfair when he got eight coins on the target but got only 17¢, whereas his opponent got only four coins but had 31¢. They decided to give a point for more coins and a point for the larger amount in each round.

Challenge the children to tell all the different amounts they could have if seven coins land on the target. There are many other problems that you and the children can make up that use this game as a basis.

Can you tell who won if Flora got five coins and Bill got four coins on the target and they each got more dimes than pennies?

Children may be at different levels when playing the game. Have grouping materials or tens and ones available for those who need to represent the numbers with concrete objects.

Later, you may want to investigate with the class what combination of pennies and dimes happened most often.

WHO WINS?

Get ready. The purpose of this activity is to have children play a game of chance, which they will analyze in the What Number? activity below.

Each group of four students will need some way to generate randomly the numbers from 1 through 4: a spinner with spaces marked 1-4, a deck of cards with only the 1-4 cards, a die marked 1-4 (with two blanks that give another throw), or four slips of cardboard with 1-4 on them in a bag. Each group will need a sheet of paper to keep a record of their score.

To find the total, have calculators available. Children who are using concrete materials could put all the tens and ones together to find the total.

Get going. For each round of the game, each child spins the spinner twice. The first spin tells the number of tens and the second spin tells the number of ones. Each child should record what number he or she gets. At the end of the round, the child with the largest number is the winner of that round. At the end of, say, four rounds, have the children find their total score by adding all the numbers. Have the children discuss whether someone could have the largest total and not have won any rounds.

Keep going. Let the children come up with their own way to keep score—the person with the smallest number, the person with the number nearest to 22, or the person who had the number nearest a number he or she chose before spinning wins the round.

Change the type of spinner to the challenge spinner shown in the illustration. Discuss with the children what happened with the challenge spinner.

Each number has an equal chance of occurring, but let the children come to that conclusion after they have gathered the data. Some children may think that 44 (or 11, 22, or 33) won't occur as often, since it has the same two digits and getting two 4s in a row is not as likely. Remember that this is just an introduction to probability; children are only beginning to build concepts.

Starting spinner

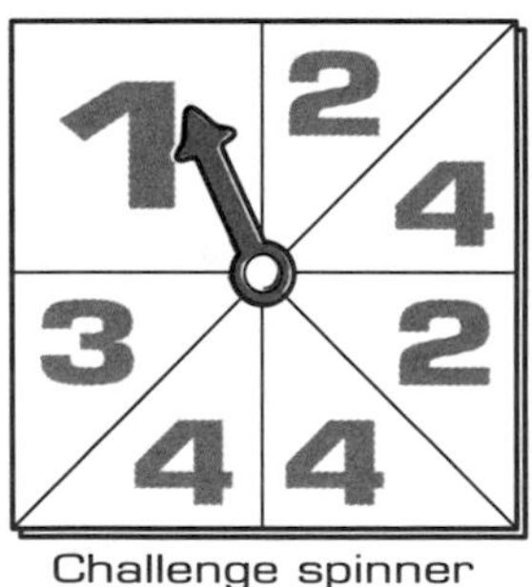

Challenge spinner

What number occurred most often? Would you be more likely to get a 22 or a 32? A 22 or a 33? A 34 or a 14?

WHAT NUMBER?

Get ready. The purpose of this activity is to have children explore the question of what number occurs most often in the Who Wins? game above. The children will be introduced to the stem-and-leaf chart as an easy way to record lots of data. The chart is set up in terms of tens and ones to emphasize place value.

Each group of four students will need some way to generate randomly the numbers from 1 through 4, such as the regular spinner in the previous activity.

Get going. Ask the children if when they played the Who Wins? game, they noticed whether 22 was spun more than 34 or if any number was spun a

♦ ♦ ♦ ♦ ♦ ♦ ♦ ♦

lot. Tell them that together they are going to try to see what happens when they all spin.

Have each child spin once for tens and once for ones and record the number. Then collect all the data (the numbers) from the class in a chart like the one shown. As a child calls out his or her number, say 23, write a 3 in the ones column in the row that shows 2 tens. This will go quickly because at this point you will not be trying to organize the data.

When all the numbers have been collected, ask the children to tell what the chart means. See if they understand by asking such questions as these:

How many students got a 32? How can we tell from the chart?

What was the smallest number?

TENS	ONES
1	2 3 1 1 3 4 4 1 2
2	2 1 1 3 3 3 1 4 2 4
3	3 3 1 4 2 2 3 1 4 1 1 4 3
4	2 2 4 4 1 3 3 1 2 3 1

Ask the children if they can quickly tell how many people got a number larger than 23. Then, show them that reorganizing the chart makes it easier to answer questions such as these:

TENS	ONES
1	1 1 1 2 2 3 3 4 4
2	1 1 1 2 2 3 3 3 4 4
3	1 1 1 1 2 2 3 3 3 3 4 4 4
4	1 1 1 2 2 2 3 3 3 4 4

How many people got 31?

How many of you got a number with a 4 in the ones place?

How many got a 3 in the ones place?

Did one number occur more often than any other?

Return to the original question: Does it look like one number is being spun more often than any other? Discuss why they think that. You may want to repeat the activity once or twice to let them see that it does not look as if any one number is being spun most often.

Keep going. Change the type of spinner to the challenge spinner shown in the previous activity and repeat the experiment.

The evaluation standards propose that student assessment be an integral part of instruction. If the stem-and-leaf chart is too abstract for most of your children, you may want to use a graph like the one below to show how many of each number:

X				X		X	
X	X	X	X	X	X	X	X
X	X	X	X	X	X	X	X
11	12	13	14	21	22	23	24

X		X					
X		X	X	X	X	X	
X	X	X	X	X	X	X	X
X	X	X	X	X	X	X	X
31	32	33	34	41	42	43	44

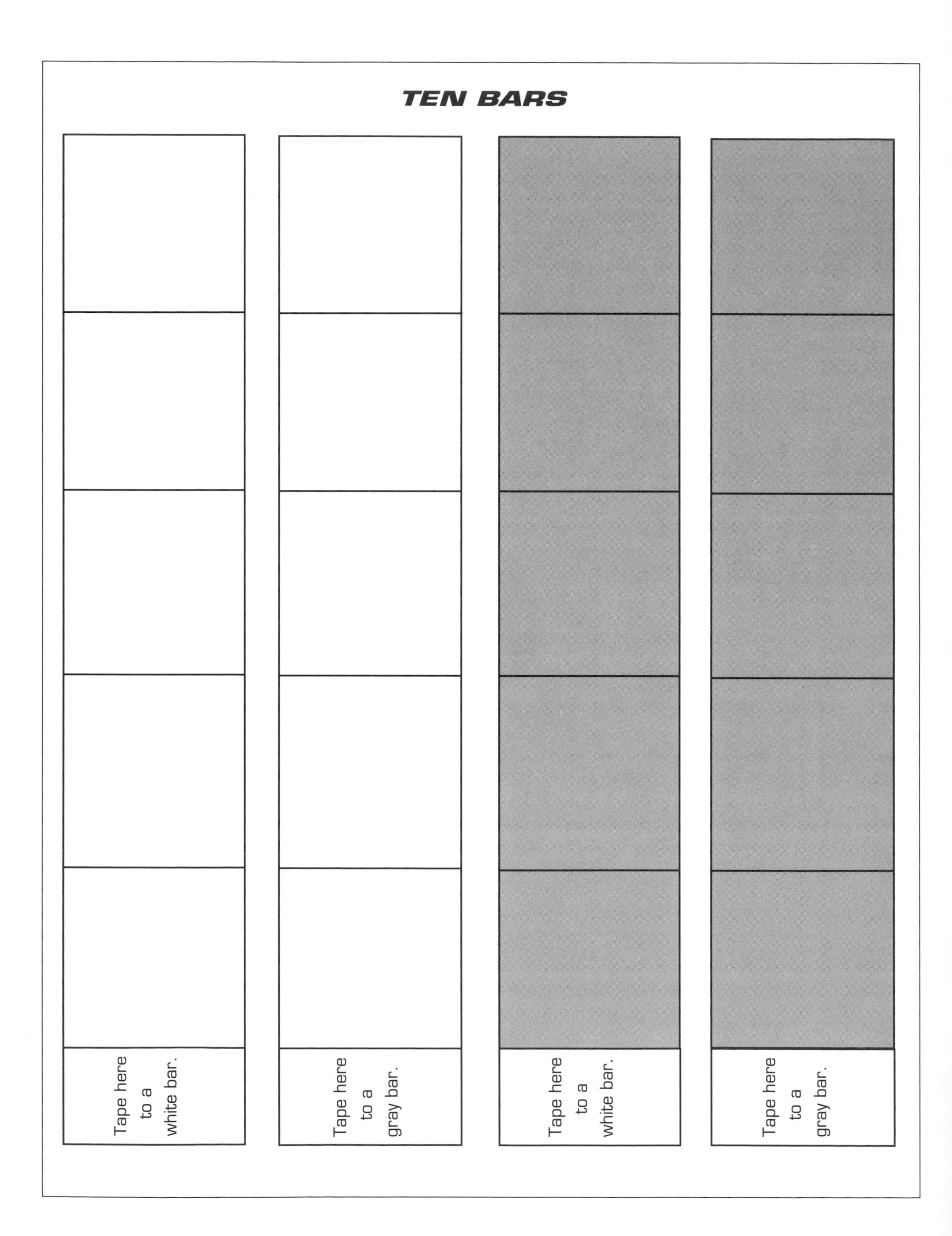
TEN BARS
Tape here to a white bar.
Tape here to a gray bar.
Tape here to a white bar.
Tape here to a gray bar.

GEOMETRY AND SPATIAL SENSE

Young children should explore geometric concepts informally and intuitively. The use of manipulatives is crucial. Sorting and classifying geometric figures in many ways provides children with informal analyses of the properties of these figures before the more formal work in later grades.

Constructing two-dimensional and three-dimensional figures with a variety of materials (blocks, geoboards, pegboards, straws and pipe cleaners, tagboard) helps children identify specific characteristics of each figure, including the symmetries of figures and some relationships between two-dimensional and three-dimensional figures. Free experimentation with such materials often leads children to investigate more than the traditional cube, rectangular prism, square, circle, triangle, and rectangle. Exploring their surroundings for examples of these figures shows the students a wide variety of geometric figures other than the ones pictured in their textbooks. Geometry activities beyond the content of this booklet are needed to help children acquire the necessary concepts.

At the first level in the hierarchy of learning geometry, "Geometric figures... are recognized by their shape as a whole, that is, by their physical appearance, not by their parts or properties. A person functioning at this level can learn geometric vocabulary, can identify specified shapes, and given a figure, can reproduce it." (NCTM 1987, p. 2)

Although some children of this age are beginning to be comfortable handling a pencil, others still find it a great chore. For that reason, few of the suggested activities demand extended use of one. Drawings that the children make should be freehand.

MAKING PLANE AND SOLID FIGURES WE KNOW

Get ready. The purpose of this activity is to have children construct models of familiar plane (two-dimensional) and solid (three-dimensional) regular figures. Children should have explored three-dimensional figures and identified edges and corners before doing this activity.

Some materials that can be used to make plane and solid figures are toothpicks with plasticine, tiny marshmallows, or frozen peas and straws with pipe cleaners or paper fasteners. Straws can be joined to form two-dimensional figures with string, paper clips, or pipe cleaners. Joining with pipe cleaners is illustrated below. Regular straws can be used full length or cut to any desired length. It is best to use narrow straws. Pipe cleaners can be used full length or cut.

At the next level in the hierarchy, "An analysis of geometric concepts begins.... Figures are recognized as having parts and are recognized by their parts." (NCTM 1987, p. 2)

Another way to join straws by using pipe cleaners is to form loops with pieces of pipe cleaner, push the ends into straws, and fasten the loops together with paper fasteners, as illustrated. When three straws are joined at a corner, a single pipe cleaner can be bent as shown and inserted in the straws.

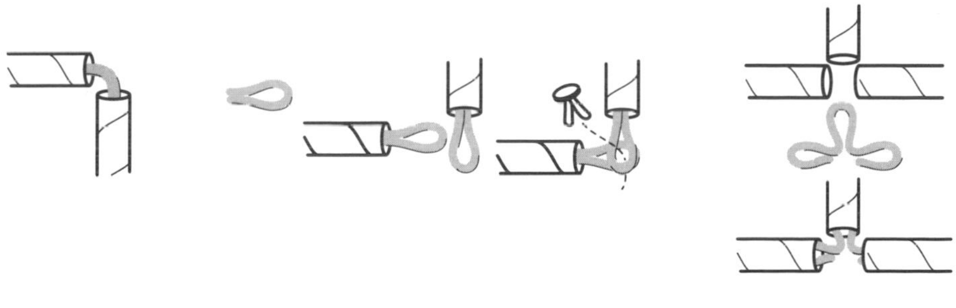

Wooden or plastic models of the figures should also be available.

♦ ♦ ♦ ♦ ♦ ♦ ♦ ♦

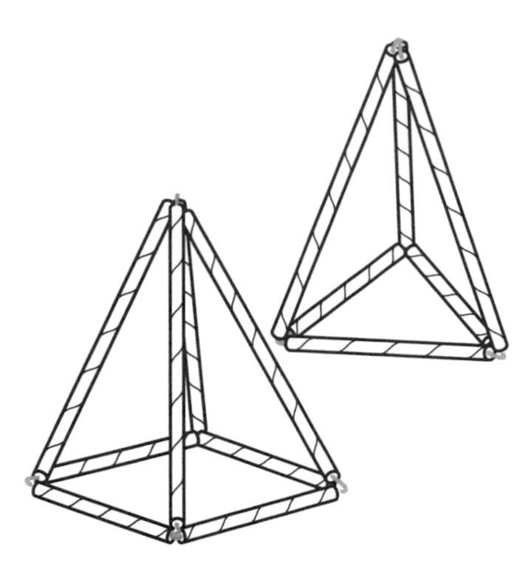

Get going. Ask the children to make a triangle, a square, a rectangle, a four-sided figure that is not a square or a rectangle, and a five-sided figure. Let the children experiment and create figures of their own.

Show the children a cube and ask them to make a model of it. Let them try it on their own and help them if needed.

Show the children a tetrahedron and ask them to describe each face and the number of straws that would meet at each corner. Ask them to make a model of the tetrahedron.

Let the children experiment to see what other models they can make.

Look at a square-based pyramid. How many edges does it have? How many edges meet at each corner?

Make a square-based pyramid by using straws and pipe cleaners. How are square-based pyramids and tetrahedrons the same? How are they different?

Repeat the preceding activity for other solids, such as different-shaped boxes and pyramids. Glue colored paper to the straws to make faces. These ornaments can be hung from the classroom ceiling.

Further ideas can be obtained from the Arithmetic Teacher***—for example, "Flexible Straws" in the November 1989 issue.***

Note: Models of solids made from straws or other similar materials are frequently called **skeletons of the solid,** a term you may wish to use.

ILLUSTRATING SLIDES, FLIPS, AND TURNS

Get ready. The purpose of this activity is to have children illustrate slides, flips, and turns. Slides, flips, and turns are physical motions encountered by students as they move objects and themselves in everyday activities. These motions are basic for understanding the properties of geometric figures in the early grades.

For this activity you may use the children themselves or several stuffed animals and 3 x 5 cards or small pieces of tagboard.

Have the students draw on one side of a 3 x 5 card a picture showing themselves lying face up; on the other side of the card they should draw themselves lying face down. Have them repeat the drawings on a second card and write their names on their cards. Each child should have two cards.

To develop spatial sense, children must have many experiences that focus on geometric relationships; the direction, orientation, and perspectives of objects in space.... (NCTM 1989a, p. 49)

Get going. Have the children lie on the floor (on their backs or on their stomachs) and ask them to give their interpretation of a slide.

How would you show a slide?

Some may slide forward, others may slide backward, and still others may slide sideways. Discuss which types of slides are the easiest.

If your head is pointing towards me to start, where is it pointing after a slide? [Same way]

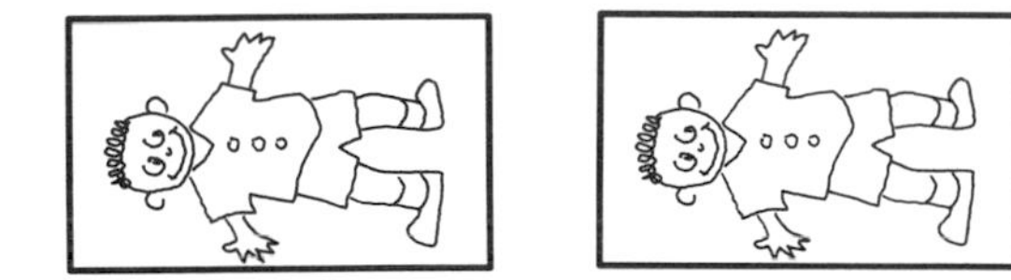

Slides

Have the children lie on the floor and give their interpretation of a flip. (In a flip, students move from their backs to their stomachs or from their stomachs to their backs.) You might suggest that they flip about their left sides, flip about their right sides, and flip about their feet.

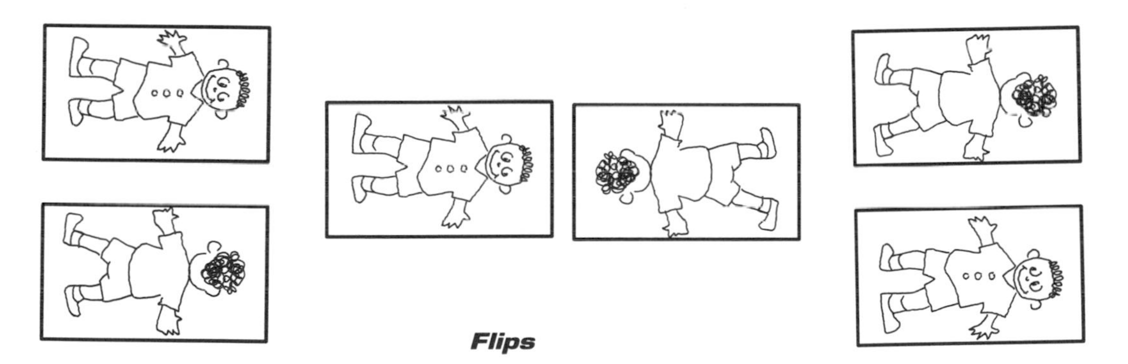

Flips

Is a somersault a flip?

Are some of these motions easier to do than others? If your head is pointing to me to start, where is it pointing after a flip? [For a right or left flip, the head will be pointing the same way; for a head or feet flip, the head will be pointing in the opposite direction.]

Have the children lie on the floor and ask them to demonstrate a turn. (The amount of turn is arbitrary at this point.)

How would you show a turn?

If moving from back to stomach is a flip and not a turn, what does a turn look like? Are your bodies pointing in the same direction before and after a turn? [No, the direction is different for all turns except for a complete turn.]

Ask the children to sit in a large circle and demonstrate the different possibilities for a slide, for a flip, and for a turn, using their cards or stuffed animals.

Discuss how all slides are alike. [You point in the same direction; you stay on your back or stomach.] Discuss how all flips are alike. [You move from stomach to back or from back to stomach but may not always point in the same direction.]

Discuss how all turns are alike. [You stay either on your back or on your stomach. You usually point in a different direction.]

Keep going. Ask the children to describe the motion that would take them from a start (initial position) to a finish (final position). Use cards to illustrate many such situations that require one move. Some examples are illustrated.

Repeat, using situations that require two moves or three moves.

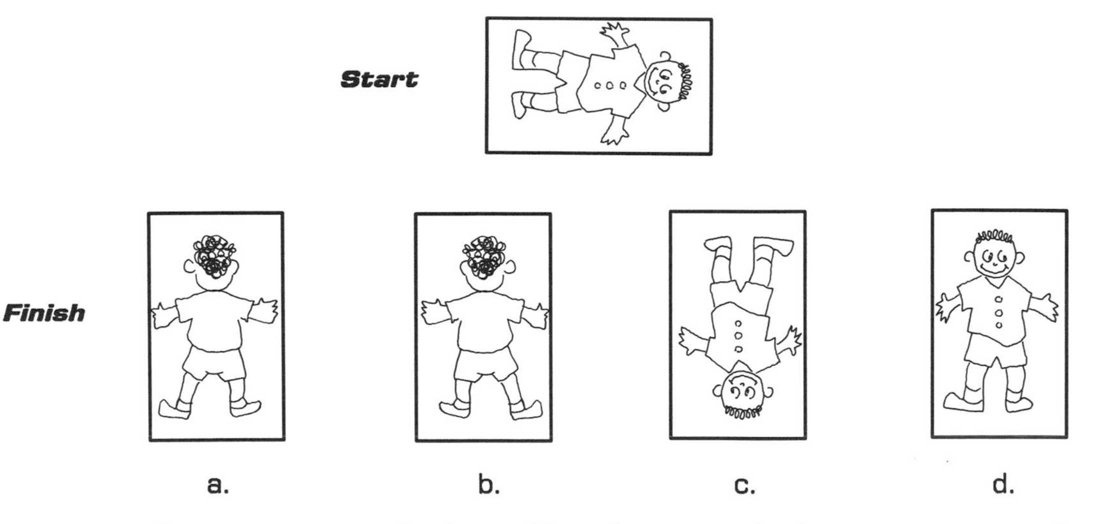

If you start on your back, would you be on your back or on your stomach after two flips? [On the back]

How would you be lying after three flips? [On the stomach]

How would you be lying after a slide, a flip, and a slide? [On the stomach]

USING A MIRROR

Get ready. The purpose of this activity is to have students become familiar with finding reflection images in a mirror and recognizing that a figure and its image have the same size and shape (are congruent). This activity helps children visualize mirror images and is an introduction to line symmetry of a figure.

Pattern blocks, dot paper, gummed circles or counters, and two silvered mirrors are needed for each pair of students.

Get going. Ask the children to draw a line segment by using a ruler. Tell them to place their mirrors on or near the line segment so that they see a longer segment, a shorter segment, a segment the same length as the given segment, or two line segments.

Can you show at least two ways to see two line segments? Are the two line segments the same length (congruent)?

Ask the children to draw a two-car train and to place their mirrors on or near it so that they can see a train four cars long, a train three cars long, a train two cars long, or a train with only one car.

Can you make a train five cars long by using only one mirror?

Have the children draw three circles or use gummed stickers or counters.

Place your mirror on or near the circles so that you see (a) six circles, (b) five circles only, (c) four circles only, (d) three circles only, (e) two circles only, and (f) one circle only.

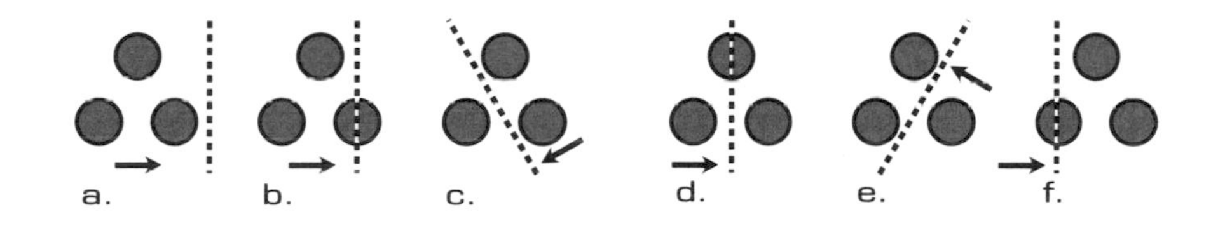

The arrows indicate the direction from which to look.

Have the children draw a square on dot paper or use a pattern block.

Use your mirror and the square to make the following figures: (a) two squares (Are the squares the same size and shape?), (b) a rectangle, (c) the largest rectangle you can make, and (d) a smaller square.

In how many ways can you place the mirror on the square and make a figure the same as the original square? [Four ways; place the mirror along lines of symmetry of the square (fig. e)]

What other figures of different shapes can you make using your mirror? [Kite-shaped figures (fig. f)]

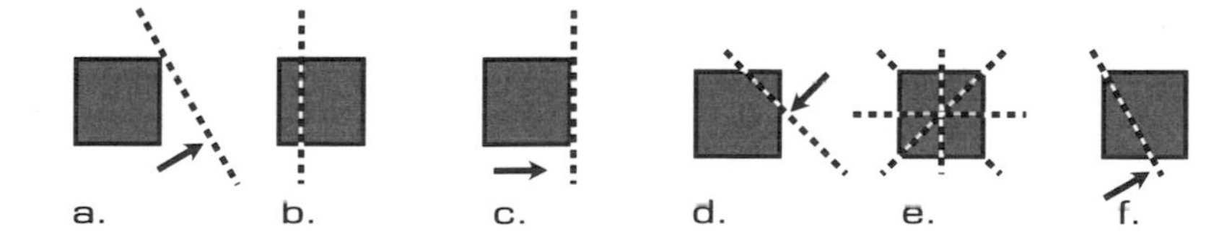

Instruct the children to use pattern blocks to make the design at the right by using a hexagon with a rhombus and a triangle on top. Guide them in placing their mirror on or near the design to see each of the following figures.

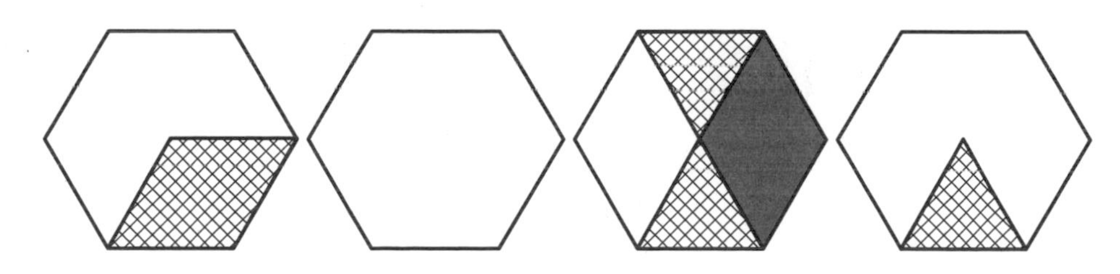

In how many different ways can you place a mirror on a hexagon so that you see a hexagon the same size and shape? [Six ways]

Place your mirror so that you see two hexagons. Are they the same size and shape (congruent)? [If the mirror is placed near but not on the hexagon, two hexagons will be seen that are the same size and shape—the original and the mirror image.]

Keep going. Show the children how to tape together two mirrors along one edge.

Make a design using pattern blocks. Place the mirrors so that the design just fits between the mirrors. What figures can you see?

Explore a variety of designs with the students. Have them remove the mirrors and try to complete the design, using pattern blocks. They can replace the mirror from time to time to check their progress. Encourage the children to alter the angle between the mirrors and explore the results.

COVERING A REGION

Get ready. The purpose of this activity is to have children cover a region completely with a set of congruent figures.

The "attribute" to be measured is area. In order to understand this concept, children need experience in covering a specific region. Using a variety of figures to cover a region helps children understand that different units may be used and that the number used to define the area depends on that unit.

Children need the attribute to be measured as well as what it means to measure. Before they are capable of such understandings, they must first experience a variety of activities that focus on comparing objects directly, covering them with various units, and counting the units. (NCTM 1989a, p. 51)

This activity shows that there is a strong connection among geometry, spatial sense, and measurement. By finding the area, we find the number of units needed to cover a given region. The units consist of geometric figures; in covering a region with these figures the child must mentally manipulate (flip and turn) the figure to fit in different positions—an ability categorized as spatial sense.

Materials required for this activity include dot paper, pattern blocks, a pattern for a square, paper, scissors, and a copy of the Cover and Count worksheet (p. 32).

Get going. Give the children three squares (pattern blocks or cut-outs) and ask them to make as many different figures as they can by joining the squares edge to edge. Ask them to compare their resulting figures with those of other students and to discuss their solutions.

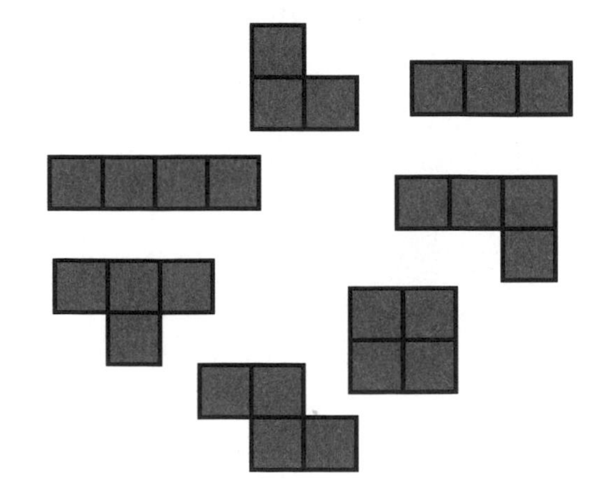

Repeat, using four squares. Ask them to draw on dot paper the figures they get. Have a student put his or her drawings on the bulletin board and ask other students to compare their figures with the ones posted.

Are any of the figures different? Do you have figures that are not already on the board?

This activity allows the children to compare figures in different orientations and, through discussion, to determine which figures are congruent (the same size and shape).

Allow the children to repeat the activity, using three or four triangles, hexagons, rhombuses, or trapezoids from the pattern blocks to make as many different figures as they can. Divide the class into groups, and let each group explore one set of figures, talking about what they discover.

How could you prove that 2 of these ◢ can cover the same area as 1 of these ■?

Keep going. Give each pair of children a pattern (template) for a square. They should each draw and cut out at least ten squares. Show the students how to cut a square into two right triangles. Discuss the idea that two of these triangles have the same area as one square. Have them cut five of their squares into right triangles.

Let the children explore with their triangles and squares the many different designs they can make to show an area of two, three, or four squares. Encourage them to make designs using different numbers of squares and triangles and then determine the area in terms of their squares and triangles. The children can show their designs on the overhead projector, record them on dot paper, and create for each other puzzles that fit the size of the squares you have given them. They might glue their designs to construction paper and make a bulletin board display.

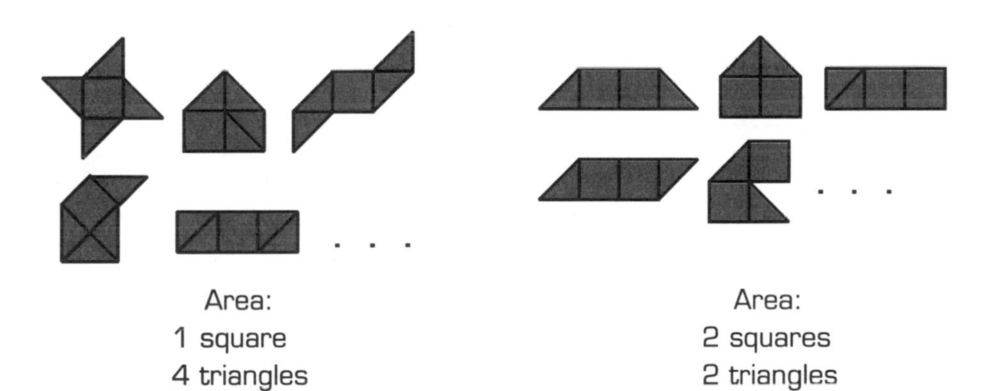

Have the students complete the Cover and Count worksheet. Children wish to draw the individual tiles in each case to help them count. This is especially needed for the nonrectangular tiles. Children may also wish to draw other outlines on dot paper for their classmate to fill in. In each case, the authors of a problem should write the answer on the back of the problem.

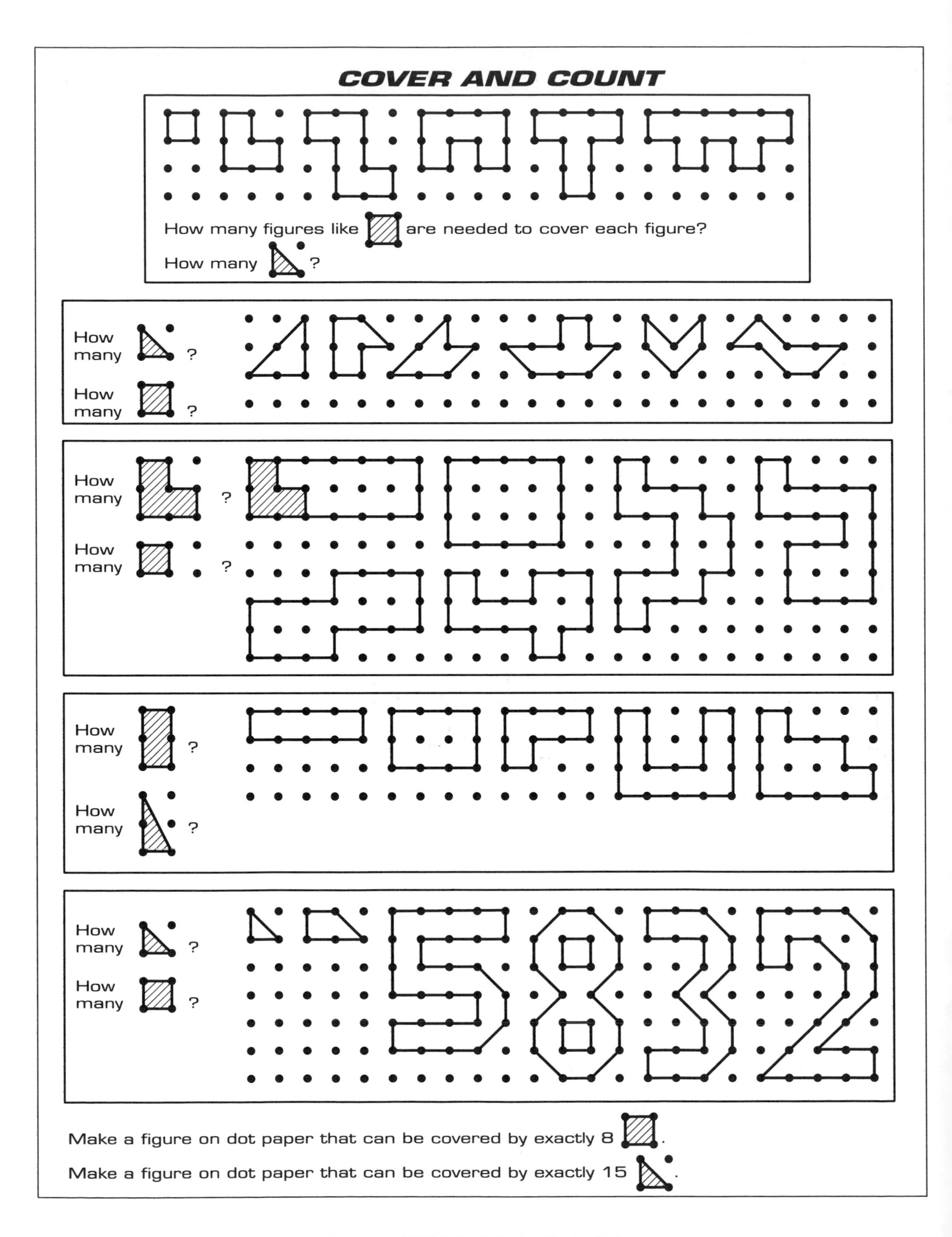
COVER AND COUNT
How many figures like are needed to cover each figure?
How many ?
How many ?
How many ?
How many ?
How many ?
How many ?
How many ?
How many ?
How many ?
Make a figure on dot paper that can be covered by exactly 8 .
Make a figure on dot paper that can be covered by exactly 15 .